Shifting Paradigms For Women Seeing Yourself Through New Eyes Instructor's Guide

by

LuVara R. Prudhomme

Copyright © 2016, LuVara R. Prudhomme. www.yourmindshift.com

All rights reserved. No part of this book may be reproduced, stored, or transmitted by any means— whether auditory, graphic, mechanical, or electronic—without written permission of both publisher and author, except in the case of brief excerpts used in critical articles and reviews. Unauthorized reproduction of any part of this work is illegal and is punishable by law.

ISBN 978-0-9908859-5-5

FOREWORD

Shifting Paradigms Series is the good news that answers so many dark questions of life that so often overshadow ones dreams and bankrupts their faith account. This guide is a balance of personal experience, backed by a biblical foundation that seals the power to apply.

Each of us who take on the challenge to use this instructive guiding light of hope to illuminate misguided pathways and increase self-awareness are empowered to shift the platform of our outlook on life. This shining moment could not have presented itself at a greater time than now.

LuVara's universal, personal and Christ-centered experiences afford her the ability to unleash a dramatic outlook on the core of life and the human process that leads to personal inventory. Readers are given a chance to fill in the blank spaces within their own lives. This is what I call "turn the corner of life", where the reader is brought to the well to drink of the author's rich experience but leave with a taste of their own as their pail of reality is drawn from the well of life.

We are thankful for her tenacity to release the God given gift so that others may be blessed as she pushes the margin and raises the bar on life's greater expectations. By allowing God to push and guide her pen to produce the life rays of hope that beams into the lives of others, her work unearths the treasure deep within.

It has been my privilege to interact with LuVara through her efforts to address the issues as is. Through the art of keeping it real, the facts and feelings are attached to real life experiences that echo the silent voice of so many.

Be prepared to find the rich blessing that lies within the rows of each chapter new mercies day by day. I declare that this book is the springboard that propels your thinking, enriches your life and shifts your paradigm.

Bishop Melvin Brown

Pastor, My Father's House
Ministries

INSTRUCTOR'S CORNER

Shifting means to change or to cause (something) to change to a different opinion, belief, etc.

A **paradigm** is a theory or a group of ideas about how something should be done, made, or thought about.

Shifting Paradigms is to change your beliefs about the way you think, the things that you do or how you make decisions. That is the aim of this book to make students take a second look or in some cases maybe a first look at themselves and everything that affects them: home, environment, relationships, and future.

The Objective of this guide is to create a starting point for each student to carefully examine where they are currently, realize the mistakes or wrong turns they have taken, devise steps or plans to come out of their situation physically or mentally, build a new plan for her life, put the plan in place, work it, re-examine it, and fine tune it until this type of living becomes ingrained and habitual. These steps can be applied to every area of life (Christian lifestyle, job, relationships, health, etc.)

It is imperative that the student feels she can expose herself to the group. Feelings will be very important at the initial sharing stages. As a leader, you must establish a trusting and open environment that is non-judgmental and allows for self-expression. Ways that you can establish this environment is by:

- Having students recite a pledge before each class.
- After each student shares, have those that can identify or share similar feelings raise their hands and allow sharing time.
- Before students are dismissed reaffirm some of the feelings that were shared (speak directly to the feeling at this point) use phrases like "it is understandable that anyone would feel ....when...........happened to them"

Each segment should be filled with affirmation of God's love, mercy and forgiveness but do not leave out redemption through repentance otherwise you will unintentionally convey to the student that God is okay with a lifestyle of sin and this will not foster change and growth. It is important that you use the Bible and find examples of God's love, forgiveness and provision in similar situations. Try to use situations that involved women so the student can relate.

When you are going through this guide you will see TOOTLIFEST, that stands for "the object of the lesson is for each student to" and then you will see the objectives. This is not all inclusive but used in conjunction with your bible, your life experiences and other techniques will be a great starting point.

As the students go through each chapter it's imperative that they are open and honest and really take time to work through each area that's covered and assess their individual lives. Take time to allow them to reflect and share. I only included 10 chapters in the book because I didn't want it to feel overwhelming and the focus be on completion. Each lesson can be broken into as many class sessions needed so students can take time to really absorb the information and be able to apply it. This slow pace will allow them to fully participate and share in thoughtful and relevant dialogue that will not only strengthen the bond between the students but will also allow everyone's voice to be heard and story to be told. Take your time going through the course; it's built to take 16 weeks but may be shorter or longer depending on the class size.

It will be helpful while they are opening up and exposing themselves that you also expose some things to the class. When writing this guide, God reminded me that He did not save, deliver or heal us just for ourselves but so we can use our experiences to help someone else avoid it or come through it. Healing starts with sharing.

I will be praying for you because it is challenging to help people overcome the past and the pain and even believe that there is something better in store for them or that there is any hope in their future. I know that you are up to the task and God will give you the grace and the determination to make a difference in the lives of the women who sit under your teaching.

I'd like to pray for and agree with you.

Dear God,

I thank you for this awesome and obedient woman of God. Father allow the oil of your anointing to flow from her to her students as she teaches them how to be in relationship with you and live a lifestyle that is pleasing to you. Let healing and deliverance take place, let strongholds and generational curses be broken. I ask that you allow the words that flow from her lips to be powerful and transformative. Holy Spirit illuminate these inspired lessons for her and allow her to teach with power and authority. Father, as she touches others' lives I ask that you touch her life in a mighty way. I pray that you strengthen her walk with you and that you order her steps. Put a hedge of protection around her everywhere that she goes and rebuke the devourer for her sake. Let her be blessed in the city, and in the field; as she goes out and when she comes in. I ask that you give her a peace that surpasses all understanding and give her more than she can ever ask or think. It is in the matchless name of Jesus Christ that we pray. Amen

I'd love to hear from you, please write me with any comments, questions or testimonies at info@yourmindshift.com

Your Sister in Christ,

LuVara R. Prudhomme

Sample Class Agenda

- Welcome

- Icebreaker/Introductions

- Housekeeping (exits, bathrooms, smoking area, food/beverages, etc.)

- Establish Norms (Only focus on yourself, Respect each other, Don't interrupt or over talk, Agree to disagree, Don't ridicule, Share)

- Break

- Overview of Course
  - Course is 4 weeks long, 2 hours each class
  - Course covers past, present and future
  - Students must come to class prepared (read chapters of the book, do worksheets, etc.)
  - Students can also go on-line to interact with others taking the course (participation and attendance will still be expected in class)
  - Attendance: Students can miss no more than 1 class for satisfactory completion of the course

- Pass out folders
  - Sister's Keeper Covenant (must be signed by each student)
  - Syllabus
  - Course Entrance Survey
  - Info for on-line portal

- Have students fill out Course Entrance Survey and return to facilitator

- Depending on venue/time etc. coffee, snacks, etc. may be served

Introduction

I believe, Dear Student, that it is no coincidence that you picked up this book. It was written just for you. There is something that is said here or a shared experience that will allow you to receive the healing and deliverance that you need to live a full and whole life. God ordained it this way. This book is a pit stop on the road to your destination; you can be fed, refreshed, refueled, and strengthened for the rest of your journey.

As you go through each chapter it's imperative that you are open and honest and really take time to work through each area that's covered and continually assess every area of your life. There may be things that you are uncomfortable with and don't want to think about or share with others but healing and deliverance starts with exposure.

I'm learning this even more as I write this book. I am a talker, I love talking but I am not a sharer; I do not share my life or experiences with others. I have a therapist for that. You won't find me in the grocery store talking to a stranger about anything personal. Although when I'm out and about many strangers talk to me about their personal lives. I can have a conversation with someone for hours and that person will leave not knowing any more about me than when the conversation began. I, on the other hand, will know their whole life story.

Maybe you're wondering why I'm telling you this. I first started writing this book in 2012. Bishop Melvin Brown of My Father's House Ministries in Charleston, South Carolina asked me to put something together for a women's mission. The church had started ministering in a low income apartment complex for women and children. I greatly admire and respect Bishop Brown and was excited that he'd asked me so I immediately started working on Shifting Paradigms. I was doing pretty good, had an outline and the first chapter completed when news came that one of my favorite uncles had died. I was very sad. After coming back from attending his funeral in Louisiana I didn't feel like writing anymore. When you write you're kind of in your own head and I needed a break from thinking. About 6 months later one of my great aunts died. I had great respect for my aunt and had actually followed in her footsteps by getting a master's degree in Education and planning to get my Ph.D. in Education also.

Experiencing so much loss really put me off my writing game I really didn't want to continue the book because I just didn't feel like writing anymore. But God had you in mind. He knew that at this point in your life you would need the words that He inspired me to write. He knew they would be relevant and life changing for you. So although it took me over a year to start writing again, it' all in God's perfect timing because the day that this book hits your hand is the day that your life will begin to change.

When I started to write again God spoke to me and said "it's time for the rest of the story". It brought to mind Paul Harvey back in the day on the radio when he would take you a little deeper into a news story and his tagline was "and now the rest of the story". I started having visions of speaking before crowds of women, which really didn't bother me but what bothered me is that I was telling them things that I would only tell my therapist. Every time I would envision myself speaking to the crowd I would be letting all of my secrets out of the bag. I was exposing myself. I talked to God about this because I felt I could be effective without having to share my life so openly with others. I have preached and taught for years but I haven't had to tell all of my business. From time to time the Holy Spirit would move me to share with someone and I would give them a piece of my testimony and that was okay but I was not okay with this tell all.

I really tried to convince God that it wasn't necessary for me to share personal things to be effective, I stopped having the visions so I felt maybe I'd made headway. Plus, I hadn't been invited to any speaking engagements anyway so I decided that I'd cross that bridge when I got to it. Needless to say that was not God's plan. He wanted me to tell the rest of the story here in this book. Every chapter that has anything about my personal life in it was written after I thought I had completed the book. During my review, I began to add more to some of the chapters and the more I wrote the more I opened my own life. God said to me, "How can you relate to them if they don't know your story?" How will they know that you've sat where they sit, in grave clothes, surrounded by ashes, wanting to lie down and give up, considering suicide, even contemplating homicide, feeling so down and so low that it took all of your strength just to lift up your head. He reminded me that I was trying to be strong, trying to be everything for everybody but neglecting myself. I looked like I had it all together but I was really empty, lonely and dissatisfied. I didn't know how I would make it but I decided to live for Him and I made it. He also said, "You are an overcomer, you broke through the pain, the depression and the disappointments and you live victoriously."

I remembered that God did not save, deliver or heal me just for me and what was the point of going through all of that hell if I wasn't going to use it to help someone else avoid it or come through it. I did not come to this easily and I wasn't as resigned as I may sound; I was still kicking and screaming. I didn't tell my entire life story but I'm glad that I did share some things because there is healing in sharing. There were still areas in my life where I needed full deliverance and as I began to write about and think about them I was able to basically "write out" the pain and hurt.

God is so amazing and awesome. He knows just what we need and how we need it. He knew that I needed more deliverance in areas that I never focus on and He knew that you needed to know that you are not alone and that there is light at the end of the tunnel. I pray that as you read this book and go through the lessons that you will begin to see your life change in a miraculous way, that you will be transformed by the renewing of your mind and allow your paradigm to shift.

To get the most out of this book I recommend that you do it in a group or at least with one other person. Hearing others' experiences can help you open up and share your own or realize that you're not alone. Being responsible to someone else also keeps you focused and on track.

If you are interested in going through the book with a group and having someone facilitate, an instructor guide is available. You will be amazed at how dynamic a group setting can be for growth and change.

Write me and let me know how this revelation and inspiration from God blesses you.

Your Sister In Christ,

LuVara R. Prudhomme

WEEK 1

CHAPTER 1

Shift My What?

TOOTLIFEST – Understand what shifting paradigms means and to determine that without changing the way that she views her past, experiences, relationships with others and relationship with God that she will not have the life that God has predestined for her.

- **Review and discuss Chapter 1**
- **Review the agenda with the students**
    - Have students take out the Sister's Keeper Covenant, read it and go around and get everyone to sign
    - Have students take out the Entrance Survey complete it and return it to you
    - Have students identify some of the areas that they know they want to change
    - Ensure students understand commitment required for the course, sign the agreement and return to you
- **Have students write down all of the obstacles that will challenge their commitment to the course; discuss and have students share possible solutions**
- **Have students write down all of their priorities and how they plan to manage those priorities during the class time; discuss and have students share possible solutions**
- **Homework:**
    - Give each student a copy of *Worksheet A, Examining Myself*, to complete and bring to next class
    - **Have students read Chapter 2, What Does My Past Say About Me**

CHAPTER 2

What Does My Past Say About Me

TOOTLIFEST-Re-examine her past, identify mistakes or derailments, examine the entire situation (age, living arrangements, relationships with parents, environment, etc.); find ways to safely let go of coping mechanisms and gain a greater understanding of the situation and its impact on the present.

LESSON I

- **Review and discuss Chapter 2**

- **Discuss repression and suppression**

  - Repression definition - Repression is the unconscious exclusion of painful impulses, desires, or fears from the conscious mind.

  - Suppression definition - Suppression is the conscious exclusion of unacceptable desires, thoughts, or memories from the mind.

  - Examine differences unconscious and conscious

  - Have students share examples of repression and suppression

- **Give each student a copy of the coping mechanisms.**

  - Talk about and give examples of ways that people employ the coping mechanisms.

  - Have students share experiences/ways they have employed coping mechanisms

  - Discuss ways students could have responded differently then, when they put the coping mechanism in place

  - Discuss ways students can let go of coping mechanism(s) now

CHAPTER 2

What Does My Past Say About Me

TOOTLIFEST-Re-examine her past, identify mistakes or derailments, examine the entire situation (age, living arrangements, relationships with parents, environment, etc.); find ways to safely let go of coping mechanisms and gain a greater understanding of the situation and its impact on the present.

LESSON II

➢ **Continue Review and discussion of Chapter 2**

➢ **Review questions from the text**

- What hurt are you still holding and pretending not to have?

- What unforgiveness are you harboring?

- Does the past overshadow your present? How?

➢ **Review *Worksheet A, Examining Myself*, with students**

- Have students share words they use to describe themselves

- Have students share mistakes

- What helps you escape the reality of your broken heart and broken dreams?

- What medication are you using for your pain?

➢ **Homework:**

- Have students Read **Chapter 3, What Does God Say About Me**

CHAPTER 3

What does God say about me?

TOOTLIFEST – Understand that God still loves her and that what has happened to her did not derail the plan that God has for her life; Recognize that God created her for relationship and fellowship.

LESSON III

- **Review and discuss Chapter 3**

  - Have students reflect on what they were doing, what they were thinking and saying and places they visited before they came to the class. (Remind them that God was there in every encounter with them). Ask if anybody wants a do-over.

  - Have students answer how many of them feel that God is always with them? How do they know?

  - Discuss ways to be in relationship and fellowship with God

  - Have students share what they feel God says and thinks about them. Ask how they know God's thoughts towards them.

  - Have students share ways that they have seen these thoughts in action

  - Discuss pain in relation to promise

  - Discuss pain in relation to purpose

  - Have students give examples of people that they know endured pain and suffering but because of those hardships they have success

  - Discuss pain and suffering

➤ **Have students define pain**

- the physical feeling caused by disease, injury, or something that hurts the body
- mental or emotional suffering: sadness caused by some emotional or mental problem
- someone or something that causes trouble or makes you feel annoyed or angry
- a warning mechanism that helps protect us by influencing us to withdraw from harmful stimuli or situations

➤ **Have students define Suffering**

- the state of undergoing pain, distress, or hardship

➤ **Discuss evolution of pain outlined in Genesis 3:**

- King James Version says I will greatly multiply thy sorrow and thy conception, pain in childbirth, pain in relationships, pain feeding yourself, the ground is cursed it will bring forth pain (thorns and thistles), pain taking care of yourself (in the sweat of thy face shalt thou eat bread) if you look at verse 21 when God made coats of skins, that's pain because that meant an animal had to be killed to clothe them. Adam also ultimately lost privileges and responsibility, and he and Eve were kicked out of their home. Disobedience brought about all of this pain
- Domino effect of pain: Romans 8:20 (the entire creation was cursed; mankind, animals, and the earth.)

➤ **Discuss effects of curse we see and experience today.**

➤ **Homework:**

- Give students *Worksheet B, Identifying My Pain*

WEEK 2

CHAPTER 4

Exposure

TOOTLIFEST – Understand that healing starts with exposure. God wants us to uncover hidden things and bring them into His light so we can be whole.

LESSON IV

➢ **Review and discuss Chapter 4**

➢ **Discuss accountability and responsibility**

- Accountability: normally to a person, organization, or institution; required or expected to justify actions or decisions; responsible; answerable, blameworthy, liable, and the expectation of giving an account to

- Responsibility: the state or fact of having a duty to deal with something or of having control over someone; answerable or accountable, as to or for something within one's power, control, or management.

➢ **Examine position vs expectations**

- Was student in a place of position (father, leader, pastor) in relationship

- Was the expectation realistic or unrealistic

➢ **Have students complete** *Worksheet C, Overcoming The Past*

- Ask for volunteers to share things owned from the past

- Discuss different ways to ask someone for forgiveness that you have hurt

- Have students write a plan for asking someone they've hurt for forgiveness

- Have students write a letter of forgiveness to two people that have hurt them

CHAPTER 4

Exposure

TOOTLIFEST – Understand that healing starts with exposure. God wants us to uncover hidden things and bring them into His light so we can be whole.

LESSON V

- **Have students complete letters of forgiveness to others**

- **Have students complete** *Worksheet E, Forgiveness*

- **Have students complete** *Worksheet D, Exposure*
  - Ask for volunteers to expose themselves to the class
  - Have students offer suggestions for healing and deliverance

- **Homework:**
  - Have students read **Chapter 5, Who Am I, for next class**

CHAPTER 5

Who Am I?

TOOTLIFEST- Be able to use descriptors that accurately identifies who she is and to help her understand who she is in Christ, to herself and to the world.

LESSON VI

- **Review and discuss Chapter 5**

- **Have students introduce themselves to the classmate next to them**

  - Students should write down the relevant things so that they can introduce the classmate

- **Discuss Identity; Identity is defined as:**

  - The distinctive characteristic belonging to any given individual

  - Who you are, the way you think about yourself, the way you are viewed by the world and the characteristics that define you

  - Ways that your identity is formed/shaped: parents and family, yourself, peers, job, relationships, positive/negative experiences, mentors,

  - This lesson will examine identity family, world, yourself, and in relation to God

- **Have students share how they were identified when they were growing up?**

  - If they had a nickname? How did they get the nick name? Do they think the nickname fit? Why or Why not? Are they still called by this nickname? Does it still fit?

  - How did you get your name?

- **Have students share 3 words that their parents used to describe them?**

- Ask how they felt about those words?
- Ask if they heard their grandparents use any of those words to their parents? How did they feel when they heard the words?

➢ **Have students discuss instances of losing or someone stealing their identity**

➢ **Have students describe situations where they acted in a way that was totally contrary to who they thought they were or what they thought they represented.**

- Have students describe a time they became what someone else wanted them to be
- Instances where the student was changed by someone else's actions
- Instances where they lost their smile; Lost their zest and drive for life
- Instances someone destroyed their dreams

➢ **Have students list their most relevant family members. Next to each person's name write what they think is the most important attribute the family member has or presents.**

- Discuss the attributes and what the student relates the attribute to
- Is it a positive or negative attribute to the student, why or why not?
- Ask the student if he has taken on the attribute of the family member, why or why not?

➢ **Have students make a list of every area of fear that they discover in their families.**

- For each area of fear that they have listed ask
  - Where it came from?
  - When did it enter into your family?
  - Through whom did it enter?

➢ **Homework:**

- Have students begin *Worksheet F, Who Am I*

CHAPTER 5

Who Am I?

TOOTLIFEST- Be able to use descriptors that accurately identifies who she is and to help her understand who she is in Christ, to herself and to the world.

LESSON VII

- ➢ **Discuss how students feel they are identified in the world**
    - Ask what role does history play, if any?
    - Ask what role does her actions/inactions play, if any?
    - How does she identify others in her race or culture?
    - How does she identify her community?
    - How does her community identify her?
    - Ask how she thinks she can change how she's being identified?

- ➢ **Review *Worksheet F, Who Am I* with students**
    - Challenge students to come up with additional characteristics
    - Challenge students to find ways to become what they desire to be

- ➢ **Ask students how they think God identifies them**
    - Have students give characteristics that they feel God uses for them
    - Discuss characteristics in relation to God's characteristics

- **Have students examine God's attributes and ways that He's identified**

    - Jehovah Jireh – Provider

    - Jehovah Rapha – Healer

    - Jehovah Tsidkenu – Our Righteousness

    - Jehovah Rohi – My Shepherd

    - El Shaddai – The Sufficient One

    - Jehovah Nissi – Our Banner

    - Jehovah Shalom – Our Peace

- **Discuss God's attributes Job 38-41**

- **Homework:**

    - Have students read **Chapter 6, Learning to Value Myself**

    - Give Students *Worksheet G, The Identified Woman*

WEEK 3

CHAPTER 6

Learning To Value Myself

TOOTLIFEST- Learn to value who she is, whose she is and her contributions to the Kingdom of God

LESSON VIII

- **Read and discuss Chapter 6**

    - Explain to each student that God values her so it is important that she values herself (as Being made in the image and likeness of God, A Woman and as a Member of the Body of Christ)

    - (Using the text, your bible and knowledge expound on these 3 areas)

    - Being Made in the Image and Likeness of God
        - Mental, physical, social and moral
    - A Woman

- **Have students choose and discuss 5 women in the Bible and point out their roles, relationship with God, characteristics, and impact.**

- **Review and discuss *Worksheet G, The Identified Woman***

    - Have students share their comments
    - Have students offer solutions and share experiences

- **Homework:**

    - Give students ***Worksheet H, Gifts! Gifts! Gifts!***

CHAPTER 6

Learning To Value Myself

TOOTLIFEST- Learn to value who she is, whose she is and her contributions to the Kingdom of God

LESSON IX

➢ **(Continued) Explain to each student that God values her so it is important that she values herself as:**
  (Using the text, your bible and knowledge expound on this area)

- A Member of the Body of Christ

    o Examine roles and responsibilities to the Body of Christ (in church, stewardship, gifts, etc.)

    o Discuss expectations and challenges

➢ **Review and discuss *Worksheet H, Gifts! Gifts! Gifts!***

- Have students share their gifts and how they can use them in the church or community

- Have students discuss gifts they aren't using and examine why they aren't using the gifts

- Have students discuss discipleship (Great Commission)/witnessing, evangelism, ministering to others

- Have students share challenges to witnessing and ways to overcome them

- Discuss Proverbs 18:16 (A man's gift makes room for him and brings him before great men)

➢ **Homework:**

- Have students read **Chapter 7, Curses**

- Give students *Worksheet I, Curses & Other Things*

CHAPTER 7

Breaking Curses

TOOTLIFEST-Realize that she can change her life by breaking curses and speaking life, and understand the benefits that God has for her

LESSON X

- ➢ **Review and discuss Chapter 7**
- ➢ **Ask students what "equals" love to them and where did that idea or thought come from?**

  Questions to ask are:

  - Does a man giving you money or taking care of you "equal" love? Why? Where did that come from?

  - Does a man giving you lots of gifts "equal" love? Why?

  - Does a man being jealous and suspicious of other men and not wanting you to go out without him "equal" love? Why?

- ➢ **Review Worksheet I, Curses & Other Things**

  - Have students expound on curses that they think are operating in their families

  - Have students share curses that they have spoken into others' lives and explain why they spoke those things

  - Have students share ways that they speak life and explain why they feel the need to speak this way

  - Have students share ways that they speak death and explain why they feel the need to speak this way

  - Have students share "self-talk" and explain why they say what they say

  - Discuss ways that students can speak life

➢ **Give students** *Worksheet J, Benefits!*

- Give students 10-15 minutes to complete the worksheet

- Review the worksheet with students; allow students to share how they define each blessing

- Ask students to give examples of ways that they feel they have received the benefits

- Ask students to also share scriptures that identify God's desire to give him those benefits

➢ **Homework:**

- Have students read **Chapter 8, Determining Who I Want To Be**

CHAPTER 8

Determining Who I Want To Be

TOOTLIFEST-Determine who she wants to be and work towards transforming herself spiritually, physically and mentally

LESSON XI

- ➢ **Review and Discuss Chapter 8**

  - Have students identify 2 people that they think have fulfilled lives and why they feel that way

  - Challenge them to ask the 2 people they selected if they are fulfilled and bring the responses back to the next class

  - Ask students if they are living a fulfilled life and to expound on why or why not

  - Ask students how they feel their lives can be fulfilling or more fulfilling and to expound on answers

- ➢ **Discuss planning with students (You will go in more detail about plans in Chapter 9)**

  - Ask students to raise their hands if they have a 5, 10, 15, or 20 year plan

  - Have students share their plans and how the plans came to be

  - Suggested discussion questions:

    o Did God give you the plan; did you ask God about the plan/have you talked to God about the plan

    o What area of your life will be affected by the plan

- Will the plan affect others; if so, negatively or positively

- Ask students what they feel is the most important aspect of the plans for their lives

- What role will God play in the plans

➢ **Discuss with students the 5 truths that we must take into consideration when looking to the future (expound in each area and have students talk about what these truths mean to them)**
  - We no longer live for ourselves but for Christ
  - We are a new creature
  - It is our responsibility to be transformed
  - We have a responsibility to others
  - God has a plan for our lives

➢ **Pick several scriptures from the chapter and discuss with students.**

  - Have students cite examples of how they can fulfill the scripture

  - Give students 10-15 minutes to work on *Worksheet K – Scriptures for Daily Living*

  - Have students share scripture and application from worksheet.

➢ **Have students take a moment to reflect on their daily lives, discuss and share**

  - Suggested discussion questions:

    - Do the people that you work with know that you have a relationship with Christ?

    - Do you affect anything in your workplace or have you been too busy focusing on yourself and your issues?

    - Do you walk in victory or are you weighed down with so many problems that many times you're the one being consoled?

    - Are you open minded to everything and everyone's lifestyle so much that no one can tell what your true values are?

    - Do you portray a live and let live attitude?

➢ **Homework:**

- Have students read **Chapter 8, Determining Who I Want To Be**

- Have students bring in *Worksheets F & G, Who Am I? and The Identified Woman*

WEEK 4

CHAPTER 8

Determining Who I Want To Be

TOOTLIFEST-Determine who she wants to be and work towards transforming herself spiritually, physically and mentally

LESSON XII

- ➢ **Continue Review and discussion of Chapter 8**

- ➢ **Read James Weldon Johnson's "The Creation" and discuss (Allow students to read the passage aloud)**

    - Expound on God's dynamo; creativity and passion

    - Focus on the importance of God creating man last (setting up provision), from dust (different from all other creation), for fellowship.

- ➢ **Have students share obstacles that hinder them from walking as a "new creature"**

    - Suggested discussion questions:

        o Do you feel that you are walking/living the way that God wants you to? Expound on responses (if so, how; if not, why not)

        o What changes do you need to make and how can you make the changes

        o Are there other influencers; if so, who are they and are they negatively or positively influencing you

- ➢ Give students **Worksheet L, My Foundation** and 15-20 minutes to complete and allow them to share

    - Tips that you can give to help students establish a foundation:

- Examine your priorities (How do you begin your day)

- What areas do you feel you need to be stronger in?

- What areas do you feel unsure about?

- What do you need most throughout the day? (i.e. peace, patience, cour- age, positive words, encouragement, etc.)

- What type of challenges do you face most and how do you handle those challenges.

➤ **Ask students about their role in the kingdom of God; allow them to share**

- Suggested discussion questions:

    - What is your role in the body of Christ

    - How do you know this is your role

    - Are you an effective member of the body ; If so, how? If not, why not

    - Do you feel responsible to other members of the body; If so, how? If not, why not

    - Do you reach out to unsaved people? If so, how? If not, why not?

    - What hinders you from reaching out?

    - How can you overcome these hindrances?

➤ **Ask students to identify themselves and share with the class**

- Suggested questions:

    - Who are you when you're not in church?

    - How do others see you? React to you?

    - What do others think about you?

- How do you dress for work? Play? Church?

- What image do you want to portray to others?

- What three words would your co-workers use to describe you?

- What are your priorities?

- How do you talk to others?

- Who is the most important person in your life? How do you convey that?

➢ **Have students compare** *Worksheets F & G,* **with** *Worksheet M* **discuss similarities and differences**

CHAPTER 8

Determining Who I Want To Be

TOOTLIFEST-Determine who she wants to be and work towards transforming herself spiritually, physically and mentally

LESSON XIII

- **Continue Review and discussion of Chapter 8**

- **Have students identify their strengths**

    - Suggested discussion questions:

        - How do you use your strengths

        - How does your strengths affect the body of Christ

        - What other strengths do you have that you don't use for Christ; why not?

- **Have students share their purpose with the class**

- **Have students share what they experienced as they changed their life-styles or began to walk in their purpose.**

- **Have students share weaning challenges that they have faced.**

- **Have students examine ways to overcome these challenges**

- **Homework:**

    - Have students read **Chapter 9, Living Purposefully**

CHAPTER 9

Living Purposefully

TOOTLIFEST – Learn how to plan and live a life of purpose and total dedication to God.

LESSON XIV

➢ **Review and discuss Chapter 9**

➢ **Give students *Worksheet N, PRAISE***

- Allow students class time to come up with at least three goals and PRAISE information for each focus area.

- Ask students to share one of their goals and PRAISE information with the class. Ensure that you ask them to share goals in different areas because this can help other students formulate goals for the focus areas.

- Remind Students that the goals and objectives don't have to be perfect, they can change, as a matter of fact they may change. This exercise will just help them get started.

➢ Homework:
- Have students read **Chapter 10, Sustaining The Shift**

CHAPTER 10

Sustaining The Shift

TOOTLIFEST – Embrace the paradigm shift that has taken place while going through this course and allow what she has learned to affect her life and everyone and everything that she comes into contact with in a profound way.

LESSON XV

- ➢ Review and discuss Chapter 10

- ➢ Give students Worksheet O, Reflections

- ➢ Have each student share at least 3 truths that they realized in the course

- ➢ Have each student share one thing that they learned from another student

- ➢ Give students Course Exit Survey and have them return forms after completion

- ➢ Pray with students

- ➢ Give students certificates for course completion

Celebrate!!!!

WORKSHEETS

Course Survey (Entrance)

Name: _____

What do you expect to gain from this course? _____

_____

_____

_____

Do you have a relationship with Christ, if so, how would you characterize it?

_____

_____

_____

What areas do you think you're weak in (i.e. walk with Christ, family dynamics, relationships, financial stewardship etc.), why? _____

_____

_____

_____

What areas do you think you're strong in (i.e. walk with Christ, family dynamics, relationships, financial stewardship etc.), why?

What would you like to change most about your life?

What are your most pressing problems right now?

How can this church/ministry help you?

SHIFTING PARADIGMS FOR WOMEN
COVENANT WITH MY SISTER

I AM MY SISTER _____ 'S KEEPER

I VOW TO:
KEEP HER SECRETS
KEEP MY COMPOSURE AS SHE SHARES
KEEP MY MIND OPEN WHEN LISTENING TO HER EXPERIENCES
KEEP MY PRIDE, ARROGANCE AND NEGATIVE OPINIONS TO MYSELF
KEEP RESPECTING HER DESPITE HER SHORTCOMINGS
KEEP ENCOURAGING HER
KEEP HER NUMBER/EMAIL AND REACH OUT TO HER
KEEP TRANSPARENCY IN OUR RELATIONSHIP
KEEP HER ABREAST OF MY CHALLENGES AND SUCCESSES
KEEP LOVING HER AS A CHOSEN AND ELECT OF GOD
KEEP HER ACCOUNTABLE TO GOD AND HER PURPOSE
KEEP HER LIFTED UP IN PRAYER

SIGNED,

_____ _____ _____

_____ _____ _____

_____ _____ _____

_____ _____ _____

COPING MECHANISMS

- Acting out: not coping – giving in to the pressure to misbehave.

- Adaptation: The human ability to adapt.

- Aim inhibition: lowering sights to what seems more achievable.

- Altruism: Helping others to help self.

- Attack: trying to beat down that which is threatening you.

- Avoidance: mentally or physically avoiding something that causes distress.

- Compartmentalization: separating conflicting thoughts into separated compartments.

- Compensation: making up for a weakness in one area by gaining strength in another.

- Conversion: subconscious conversion of stress into physical symptoms.

- Crying: Tears of release and seeking comfort.

- Denial: refusing to acknowledge that an event has occurred.

- Displacement: shifting of intended action to a safer target.

- Dissociation: separating oneself from parts of your life.

- Emotionality: Outbursts and extreme emotion.

- Fantasy: escaping reality into a world of possibility.

- Help-rejecting complaining: Ask for help then reject it.

- Idealization: playing up the good points and ignoring limitations of things desired.

- Identification: copying others to take on their characteristics.
- Intellectualization: avoiding emotion by focusing on facts and logic.
- Introjection: Bringing things from the outer world into the inner world.
- Passive aggression: avoiding refusal by passive avoidance.
- Performing rituals: Patterns that delay.
- Post-traumatic growth: Using the energy of trauma for good.
- Projection: seeing your own unwanted feelings in other people.
- Provocation: Get others to act so you can retaliate.
- Rationalization: creating logical reasons for bad behavior.
- Reaction Formation: avoiding something by taking a polar opposite position.
- Regression: returning to a child state to avoid problems.
- Self-harming: physically damaging the body.
- Somatization: psychological problems turned into physical symptoms.
- Substitution: Replacing one thing with another.
- Symbolization: turning unwanted thoughts into metaphoric symbols.
- Trivializing: Making small what is really something big.
- Undoing: actions that psychologically 'undo' wrongdoings for the wrongdoer.

WORKSHEET A
EXAMINING MYSELF

Name three words that you use to describe yourself and explain why you chose the word.

A. _____

_____

_____

_____

B. _____

_____

_____

_____

C. _____

_____

_____

_____

Name 3 of the biggest mistakes you feel you have ever made and the age you were when you made the mistake.

A. _____
_____
_____

age:____

B. _____
_____
_____

age:____

C. _____
_____
_____

age:____

Where did you live and who did you live with? _____
_____
_____

How would you describe your home/environment at that time?

For each mistake write down why you felt you made the mistake.

Mistake 1

Mistake 2

Mistake 3

Do you blame yourself for the mistake? If you do why do you blame yourself?

Mistake 1: <u>yes or no. if yes, why?</u>
_____
_____
_____

Mistake 2: <u>yes or no. if yes, why?</u>
_____
_____
_____

Mistake 3: <u>yes or no. if yes, why?</u>
_____
_____
_____

How do you feel the mistake is still affecting you now?

Mistake 1
_____
_____
_____

Mistake 2
_____
_____

Mistake 3

Which coping mechanisms did you use or are still using?

What better ways could you have responded or can respond now?

Additional Comments:

WORKSHEET B

IDENTIFYING MY PAIN

What is my pain?
_____
_____
_____

Why do I feel I have this pain?
_____
_____
_____

How do I react to the pain (i.e. cry, get angry, scream)
_____
_____
_____

What did I do or not do to contribute to my pain?
_____
_____
_____

What type of help do I need for my pain?
_____
_____
_____

What do I need to do to stop my pain?
_____
_____
_____

What's keeping me from stopping my pain?
_____
_____
_____

What changes will I have to make when my pain is gone?
_____
_____
_____

Who else is affected by my pain?
_____
_____
_____

If a Christian, what scripture addresses my pain?

WORKSHEET C

OVERCOMING THE PAST

Things that I own from my past:
_____
_____
_____

People I need to forgive for hurting me:
_____
_____
_____
_____
_____

Write a letter of forgiveness to two of the people that hurt you

WORKSHEET D

EXPOSURE

Hello My name is _____ and I_____

_____
_____
_____
_____
_____
_____
_____
_____
_____
_____
_____
_____
_____
_____
_____
_____
_____
_____
_____

WORKSHEET E

FORGIVING MYSELF

I forgive myself for

WORKSHEET F

WHO AM I?

Words that describe me: _____
_____
_____

Words that I want to describe me: _____
_____
_____
_____
_____
_____

What changes do I need to make to be described by my desired words: ___
_____
_____
_____
_____

WORKSHEET G

THE IDENTIFIED WOMAN

Who am I claiming to be? _____
_____
_____

What do I claim that my life doesn't reflect? _____
_____
_____

What am I lacking? _____
_____
_____

How do I get what I lack? _____
_____
_____
_____

What needs to be a part of my identity?

_____
_____
_____
_____
_____

How can I add these attributes to my life?

_____
_____
_____
_____
_____

What changes am I willing to make in my life/daily walk with Christ?

_____
_____
_____
_____
_____

WORKSHEET H

GIFTS! GIFTS! GIFTS!

What gifts do I have?
_____
_____
_____

What gifts am I walking/operating in?
_____
_____
_____

I'm not sure of my gifts but I am very good at:
_____
_____
_____

How can I use these areas to support my church or community?
_____
_____
_____

If I had my choice I would like my gift to be. Why?

_____
_____
_____

Last month, I operated in my gift by

_____
_____
_____

Next month, I will operate in my gift by

_____
_____
_____

I am obeying the Great Commission by

_____
_____
_____

I will make a commitment to obey the Great Commission by

_____
_____
_____

WORKSHEET I

CURSES & OTHER THINGS

What generational curses do you think are still operating in your family? Why?

_____
_____
_____
_____
_____
_____

What curses have you spoken into your own life?

_____
_____
_____

What curses have you spoken into your children's lives?

_____
_____
_____

What curses have you spoken into your husband's/significant others' life?

_____
_____
_____

In what ways do you speak life?

_____
_____
_____

In what ways do you speak death?

_____
_____
_____

Identify ways that you can curb/control your tongue?

_____
_____
_____
_____
_____

WORKSHEET J

BENEFITS!

Do you know the benefits that you have in Christ? Here are just a few, please write the definition of what you think each benefit means.

Add to the list.

Blessed

_____

_____

Highly Favored

_____

_____

Fearfully & Wonderfully Made

_____

_____

Righteous

_____

_____

Adopted

_____

_____

Sound mind

_____

_____

Grace

_____

_____

Mercy

_____

_____

Abundant life

_____

_____

Peace

_____

_____

Joy

_____

_____

Wealth

_____

_____

Father

_____

_____

Savior

_____

_____

Holy Spirit

_____

_____

Covenant

_____

_____

Eternal life

_____

_____

More than a conqueror

_____

_____

WORKSHEET K

SCRIPTURES FOR DAILY LIVING

1 Peter; 2 Corinthians 6:11-18; Romans 12:10-21; Romans 13:8-14 all outline how to have a Christian life-style. Go through the scriptures and identify those that you need to apply to your life and ways you can apply them.

Scripture:

_____
_____

Application:

_____
_____
_____

Scripture:

_____
_____

Application:

_____
_____
_____

Scripture:

Application:

Scripture:

Application:

Scripture:

Application:

WORKSHEET L

MY FOUNDATION

My daily scripture:

_____
_____
_____

Help:

_____
_____
_____

Strength:

_____
_____
_____

Guidance:

_____
_____
_____

Relating to Others:

_____
_____
_____

Peace:

Love:

Encouragement:

Character:

My Daily Plan:

WORKSHEET M

KEEPING IT REAL

Who are you when you're not in church?

_____
_____
_____

How do others react to you?

_____
_____
_____

What do others think about you?

_____
_____
_____

How do you dress for work? Play? Church?

_____
_____
_____

What image do you want to portray to others?

___

___

___

What three words would your co-workers use to describe you?

___

___

___

What are your priorities?

___

___

___

How do you talk to others?

___

___

___

WORKSHEET N

PRAISE

This is your PRAISE Plan you can use whatever alternative words you want for the acronyms.

Goal for Daily Living:

_____

_____

_____

P_____	
R_____	
A_____	
I_____	
S_____	
E_____	

Goal for Occupation:

_____

_____

_____

P_____	
R_____	
A_____	
I_____	
S_____	
E_____	

Goal for Finances:

_____

_____

_____

P_____	
R_____	
A_____	
I_____	
S_____	
E_____	

Goal for Health:

_____
_____
_____

P_____	
R_____	
A_____	
I_____	
S_____	
E_____	

Goal for Relationships:

_____

_____

_____

P_____	
R_____	
A_____	
I_____	
S_____	
E_____	

Goal for Services:

_____

_____

_____

P_____	
R_____	
A_____	
I_____	
S_____	
E_____	

Goal for Witnessing:

_____

_____

_____

P_____	
R_____	
A_____	
I_____	
S_____	
E_____	

Other Goal:

_____

_____

_____

P_____	
R_____	
A_____	
I_____	
S_____	
E_____	

WORKSHEET O

REFLECTIONS

Which lesson helped me the most, why?

_____
_____
_____
_____
_____

What did I learn that I didn't already know?

_____
_____
_____
_____
_____
_____

What did I learn about myself?

_____
_____
_____
_____
_____
_____

What other student impacted me the most, why?

_____

_____

_____

What will I take away from this course?

_____

_____

_____

_____

_____

What changes have I made since being in the course?

_____

_____

_____

_____

What plans for change have I made?

_____

_____

_____

Course Survey (Exit)

Name:
_____

On a scale of 1-10 (1 being not effective; 10 being extremely effective) how would you rate the course? _____

What do you think would make the course better?

_____
_____
_____
_____
_____
_____
_____

Do you think your relationship with Christ has changed throughout the course? If so, how? If not, why not?

_____
_____
_____
_____
_____

Were some of your weak areas focused on in the course? (i.e. walk with Christ, family dynamics, relationships, financial stewardship etc.), If so, did it help you?

_____

_____

_____

_____

_____

Were you able to gain more strength and insight in your strong areas (i.e. walk with Christ, family dynamics, relationships, financial stewardship etc.), If so, in what ways?

_____

_____

_____

_____

_____

_____

What do you think has changed in your life since going through the course?

_____

_____

_____

Were your most pressing problems addressed? If so, how? If not, why not?

_____

_____

_____

_____

_____

Did the group setting help you? If so, how? If not, why not?

_____

_____

_____

_____

_____

Additional comments

_____

_____

_____

_____

_____

Thank you for filling out the survey, this information will be used to improve our program and will be shared with course facilitators and group leaders.

www.ingramcontent.com/pod-product-compliance
Lightning Source LLC
Chambersburg PA
CBHW060457300426
44113CB00016B/2628